Healing in the dark

This is more for me than you

A L Winters

This book is pretty much unedited

This book is exactly how I want it

This is raw

This is me

And this is how I speak

Some poems in this book might be triggering

I hope you enjoy

1.

I danced around you believing I was your world

In your arms you held me as I twirled

Everything around us would disappear

With everything I had I held you near

I felt your fingers start to slip

I came back confused by the rift

Only to find you facing away

Laughing I asked if this was a new game

No words came out of your mouth

To be up so high and then slammed down south

I screamed and yelled

With your back still towards me I fell

No matter how much or how loud

My voice to you didnt make a sound

The more I tried to reach and grasp

The harder it got for me to grab

Now something has its hold on me

Dragging me into the surroundings I could no longer see

I felt the darkness the way it crept

Taking me away from you no matter how hard I wept

How it hurt to be cast to the edge of the universe

Especially when it was in my waters that you surfed

The darkness is now claiming what was once yours

When it came to my demise you ensured

2.

I wonder what people will think about me when I leave them behind

Would they know how hard it was and that I tried

Will they remember me smiling when it rained

My kindness that I gave away

I wonder if I'll finally be forgiven for all my mistakes

Because there isn't a single person that has met me that knew that

sometimes I lost my way

Would they think of the joy that I brought to their lives

Even though I struggled to bring joy to mine

Maybe they'll finally see that im perfect despite my flaws

Will they forgive themselves for making me feel like who I am is wrong

Perhaps they will give me the love i deserve

Or will they cherish that memory that they are so hell bent to preserve

I know that my end will be hard for some

A pain that will follow no matter how far they run

I may meet death at the final stage of life

I may meet it when my hand reaches for the knife

I don't wish to be gone tomorrow with so much left unfinished

Each day that goes my I can feel my life start to diminish

3.

Drink drink drink

Sink

Drink drink drink

Sink

Drink until I can barely see

Drink until I feel free

Some question if I have a problem

When joy is something I have been robbed from

Bring on tomorrow i fucking dare

Because I'll keep going till the suns up I don't care

Can't wait to see what the next day will bring

So with another bottle I'll take a swing

Don't mind if I hit or miss

Because everyday I'm going to feel bliss

4.

I crave you

Knowing that craving would only betray myself

To let you in

Isn't something I would call wealth

I don't need you to be here for a season

I need you for a very specific reason

To make the ache in my chest go away

To be the sun in the middle of the day

My entire soul is reaching out

Clinging to everyone about

Trust is a thing earned and not given

But it is my life and thoughts i wish to share

But to lose someone so entwined with me i cannot bare

Shouldn't of had to live through so much pain in these short years

Searching looking for the right person to care

I'm starting to think this is all and that its done

That when I took the chance i should of run

Instead I let fate get me in its grasp

And wound up like a necklace without a clasp

These bonds I try not to think they are useless

However to me that's exactly what the truth is

To be a person and love so deep

Left with nothing but tears to reap

For the time being I think I'm done

No longer waiting for anyone to come

I am alone and will remain so

Because for this season I refuse to let anything go

5.

I saved myself from the vultures

From their pecking beaks

From the claws that are on their feet

I saved myself from the darkness of the universe

From all of its hidden corners

From the endless amount ot torture

Many days my courage waivered

Drowning myself to the sound of my own screams

To put an end to me fleeing

So much discomfort in peace

When you're used to the torment

Silence deafening

When you're used to hearing your rapid heartbeat

I thought I was nothing but a voyager at sea

On a ship without a captain

And a wheelhouse without a key

Preparing for the wreck

For pieces to float from shore to shore

Covered in my blood like an endless

But I saved myself

6.

Does this even work

With every word you pick me up and but me down

Does this even work

Talking when we know we're destined to be apart

What's the point of replaying the scene

A vhs that's played and then rewound to only start over again

Like a tooth that needs to be pulled with a shit ton of aspirin

One pants leg at a time to start the journey

Pain no longer accompanied by anger and fury

Time

Time to sit in that tiny house

Time to move on and find that meadow

To sit in that tiny house

With a tea made my a tin kettle

You even hear the birds chirp when it rains

The sun always ready to come out and play

Sometimes loving yourself means creating distance

Choosing you means stepping up and making everyday different

7.

I let you touch me because I felt alone

Turns out you were talk and no show

I regret not getting up and going home

And i here i was thinking it was my turn to blow

Too bad I didn't stick with my purple flower

It would of kept me busy for at least an hour

I'm used to disappointment that i can take

However it is unacceptable from a rake

I laugh now that you think they were tears of joy

Especially since you can't compete with my smallest of toys

Now i'm just another notch on your belt

A bigger "o" than the one I felt

8.

I hid behind your touch patches of rough skin

Lying to myself knowing it's the greatest sin

I crave the softness and diving in

Diving in deep

Deep into a face full of flowers mine to keep

I don't want to smell the woods and the moss

While walking around lost

Searching for the warmth before it begins to frost

Before I freeze from unsatisfied needs

I want clear skies

I want to be the bumble bee

To feel the grass tickling my feet

The forest is full of bears that i wish to chase me

To rip me apart and devour me

Thorny bushes scratching my legs

Tonly finding foxes to lead the way

The softness of petals and the smell of roses

They are so fragile so gentle for my boldness

Oh but I crave to dive deep

Deep into the dirt underneath my feet

The resistance pushing against my hands

My fingertips feeling life within the land

Oh I hate the woods

Oh how I hate the trees

Oh how I hate how they over shadow me

9.

I know his fingertips left you confused

Crying because you`re sad and you think you`re going to get in trouble too

I get why you didn't speak up

You weren't wrong in letting him take advantage of you

He was young but you were a child too

The only difference is that he was wrong and he knew

Your innocence was left battered and bruised

While you were supposed to be learning how to tie your shoes

Now he'll always be known as the boy in the blue house

And he's forgotten all about you since you were just another mouse

But we remember the feeling of his hardness under his jeans

Barely knowing what it was much less what it means

You had a close idea when he took off your shirt so he could see

Apart of us he killed

I know you wanted to run but we weren't going to get very far fast on

training wheels

10.

I saw the pain in your eyes

And I turned blank

I ignored the pleas ignored the cries

I tried not to hurt you

And now suffering is the only thing in sight

Rimmed with tears

Cry with all your might

Shut out the light

Shut out the truth

Away you flew

From the pain

From anything attached to my name

I changed you

The curse of loving me caused you not to be the same

In me you only saw the good

Thought that would win

But it was my nature you misunderstood

A predator that cannot be tamed

A lion is still a lion even in a cage

I will always be the same

A nightmare that confirms your fears

Nothing in my path I spare

And whatever you love I'll seize to destroy

To be feared

To be seen

To be the testimony of your pandora's box

To your garden I am the fox

It is who I am

11.

I've been to hell

And I've been free

And I've been stuck behind cells

I've been down for so long they counted me out

But I just grabbed an ace from the hand I've been dealt

12.

You asked me to and I did

You wanted me to let you in

So I let my demons out

You wanted to know what plagues my brain

You're the one who wanted to know my past mistakes

Now you avoid me

I was the person you loved

And now you look at me as if I have a stranger's face

This isn't a small thing it's a journey

I take it day by day because I'm in recovery

What's that look that you're giving me

Give me some credit

I was the one who was captured

I wrecked it

And I walked out on the kingdom that tried to keep me

Have you ever wanted to taste something so bad your teeth ache

Have you ever felt so violent to the point your body shakes

Have you ever stole because you were desperate for money and spent

every hour of the day hungry

Have you ever felt you failed at life by just existing

Have you ever been so desperate for love that you gave and took

everything

Have you ever been tired of being taken advantage of so you just let it

happen

I cry now because I have no drugs to numb it

I have all these feelings and memories with no way to destroy it

I put myself in horrible situations

Praying I wouldn't live through it

I'm trying to be the person I always wanted to be

13.

When I finish sinking

Will I finally no longer be alone

To the depths of the ocean

Will I blend in with my faded bones

And I slowly let the air out

I feel heavy like a stone

My heart is open but nobody is home

The light blue water turns dark

No longer stings my wounds

Life is merciless like a shark

I'm done being consumed

I'm giving myself a break

One that life wouldn't give

I couldn't catch my breath

No matter how hard i fought to live

For those wondering

No I'm absolutely not sorry

You heard it thundering

Saw the lightning hit my body

Left in the rain

Left in the cold

Left in a place where you knew I wasn't at home

Taking advantage of my kindness

Nothing but thoughtless

Using me to feel loved

A gun pointed to my head

Always seen as the joke

Even when I wasn't laughing

On the harsh words I choked

While you ran around dancing

Don't shed a single tear for me

Because it was you that made me bleed

Like a child with scraped knees

I feel upon my feet

I've found a place for me

And I made sure to reserve my seat

A place dark and cold

Where hope no longer meets

14.

I'm drowning in open waters as if I don't know how to swim

Lungs about to burst as I meet the krakens grin

15.

You won't let me heal because you're scared I'll move on

I feel like this entire thing was just a long con

I'm starting to think you planned this

Healing this wound is more difficult than the ones on my wrist

In your mid to be without you is to not exist

I was lived before yo

And I'm willing to die without you

We both know you were ready to kill me

Like a flower stumped under your feet

I remember it was just us until there was three

Like a potted plant you couldn't keep me from growing

The agony of losing me is now showing

Now you know you I can't be replaced

Now you know I'll never love you again because it's not safe

Neither one of us is stupid enough to be catch anoter case

Neither one of us is stupid enough to think that I can be replaced

The consequence of falling in love in a haste

My feet are no longer weighed down

Though you devaluing me it was love I found

16.

I care about children

I want every single one to be born

Even if that means they live in poverty because that is nothing but a painful

thorn

It doesn't matter that schools are underfunded and understaffed

Its okay because at least pbs taught them the difference between a lion

and a giraffe

Doesn't matter that they will live with neglect

No one cares about the fact the a miserable childhood is what comes next

The point is that babies now have a life

Even if the parents can't afford to take care of their poor eyesight

Its okay that some places don't even have water

It's not worth mentioning as long as we celebrate the life of such a beautiful

daughter

Even when you're left with bathing water that would kill a flower

Their minds will bloom with horrible mental health

Despite the fact that the government has money it's known for its wealth

Political parties forcing children to be born in situation in towns they

wouldn't raise their own in

Like I said it doesn't matter what kind of life they will be thrown in

As long as there is many going to orphanages

There aren't enough faster parents but who needs

Especially when those kids end up getting beaten

They'll probably turn to drugs and alcohol

And we'll sit here wondering how is that they could have such a hard fall

I tell the women its okay that you were raped

It was god's plan no matter their mental state

Whatevef you do dont turn to suicide

After all your body carries life

Childbirth might kill you

Think of the baby even if it kills them too

I promise you there's resources that you can go to and apply

I also promise you that most likely you will be denied

Im sure your abuser will pay child support

That maybe your only option to survive so try not to think about it as a last

resort

Children are precious we should treat them so

Now let's cut funding and watch all the school sports go

17.

How did I get here I ask myself another time

Looking at another empty bottle and my head screaming why

I gave in

I gave in again

I give in to temptation

It constantly wins

I'm not going to apologize

Your tears aren't going to convince me otherwise

I'm not going to stop

Not until I drink the last drop

I won the battle against pills

Before it could take its kill

I no longer self-harm

Leaving behind evidence on my arm

With alcohol is a war I will lose

I swallow knowing it's the truth

I clean my room finding can after can

It makes me sick to my stomach

It's hard to stand

Maybe I need another drink

I swear it's been a week

Even though it was just yesterday

Another drink will help keep the sickness at bay alcohol is what makes my

world spin

I'm grabbing another bottle ready to dive in

18.

I've been taught that loving you goes against nature

Many people told me that erasing it would be as easy as saying a prayer

But I don't want to get on my knees unless it's for you

I like what I shouldn't yea it's true

I dont see whats wrong with liking color

Life without you would be duller

You make it hard to breathe

I'm fine with choking as long as it's on your release

The forbidden fruit juice trickling down my chin

I'll take the punishment for its worth this sin

I swear you feel like velvet

Tell the truth what you do to me you like it

Going down

The sex

My hand on your breast

Not giving you a second to rest

Impossible to catch your breath

With you I'll always give into pleasure

The desire runs so deep through me it's impossible to be measured

Your cries are my ultimate trigger

There's not a time were I won't surrender

Riding high after high

I'll show you just how much I love the taste of you

19.

I can't believe that's how you really feel about me

That's unreal

If you could feel the pain in my heart

Then you would know that shit kills

I've been nothing but supportive and you've been nothing but judgemental

And if you think I'm going to believe all those lies coming out of your mouth

Then you must be mental

You've made plenty of mistakes and I'm not good enough for you

You've made plenty of mistakes and I'm not good enough for you

The harder you all are on me the more I want to leave

The pressure is suffocating and I just want to breathe

I know that I'm free and when you go back to criticizing i get snappy

Ya'll hurt me so bad I hurt myself

Then you went to blame it on me and my mental health

How would you feel if your own mom calls you fat and disgusting

I was going through puberty my entire body adjusting

How would you feel if someone hurt your feelings and you were begging

them to stop

Telling you 're too sensitive and then blame you after you bottle it up and

pop

You think that being apart of this family is great

Because it makes me feel ashamed

I don't want to do family dinner especially since in your mouth is my name

You all keep telling me to get over it

Don't you think I tried

But it's your voices in my head when I want to kill myself at night

20.

I can't believe we're done

That this chapter is now complete

Even when I think about us we're not gone

There's this pain in my chest

And I wonder how our lives could of went so wrong

I promised myself I wouldn't cry over you

But in the end that's what's keeping us alive

Do you still want me

I know that we're toxic together

But this heartbreak makes it hard to breathe

It's been over a year

And I still want you next to me

I had a love that completely consumed me

And I even love the damage that it leaves

You're the first person I wanted to marry

I was the feather in the wind

It was your your love in which it was carried

I gave my soul to you

And with your words you stabbed it through

I don't think I can love like this again

I never thought I would love like this to begin with

Everyone after to you has been a disappointment

None of them a greater disappointment than what you have been

You broke me so many times

That I no longer know who I am without you

All those times I came back

Knowing you were the predator and I was the prey

Until I couldn't anymore because I knew it was always that way

Was it a shock to your soul like it was a shock to mine

Do you walk around feeling like fell into a hole and missed the big orange

sign

I hate you

I know you feel the same

It's been over a year

I have cried countless amount of tears

Do you understand what that love has done

Do you know that inside I feel like a dying sun

No matter how horrible the pain

I would do everything the same

This can't be it

I thought we were going to grow old together

Now it's just me on this porch I sit

Cupid struck it's arrow and it didn't miss

21.

You left me with haunted memories

You're the ghost of the person you used to be

I try to reach out to you

But you move like a fragment of a dream

You're stuck in the shallow end

Waiting for all of your mistakes to do you in

I saw you fall thinking you could fly

I saw how hard you hit the ground aiming for the skies

Grabbing every rush to keep you high

Company to keep all the loneliness from your mind

If you only knew the depths of which you could swim

If only you knew now what you knew back then

I saw you fade away

Cursing at god for the day you were made

You always smiled and said scars show your strength

All the while digging your own grave

If I knew then what I knew now

I would of screamed your name before you couldn't recognize the sound

I wouldn't of played all your games I would of helped you turn around

Was all this worth walking as a ghost

Was it worth losing those you loved the most

Was it worth jail and all those predicaments

Was it worth losing yourself over and over again

To walk down a path knowing the destination wasn't something we'd meet

Gripping the edge so hard that our skin bleeds

And now I can't escape this hallow side of me

22.

Fuck

I almost regret turning my life around

Now i can see my life burning to the ground

I thought I would I was better than them

This entire time I've been drowning when I thought I could swim

With me I thought these generational curses would end

Now I'm addicted to them

The alcohol and substances

The violence and toxic men

The bad decisions

The positions I put myself in

I get angry because so many people said I wouldn't win

This isn't fair

I didn't ask for this

It's something I thought that I could get away from

Turns out I'm trapped in it and then some

Mental illness has taken control

It's driving the demons I can't let go

23.

I'm looking for friendship

You want something different

You want me to give something

The one thing I can't give

I don't want to fall in love

There's red stains all over this white dove

Because the only way I know how to love is dirty

You would understand if you could see what I saw

The ocean is full of ships more sturdy

I don't want to drown in the lying and the cheating

I don't want to be silenced when i'm being me

They claim to be the broom

Knowing I would end up getting the rugged pulled beneath my feet

Relationships are the reason why I don't love myself

Does that even need to be spoken

You should be grateful that I consider you a friend

I'm fine with being alone til the very end

I hold you close and you're the reason why I'm starting to trust again

However you must be foolish if you think your love is what I need to mend

24.

Yea I did it

So what

You're honestly going to look at me like I give a fuck

25.

Life is like a rough draft

Nothing is final and it's incomplete

There's missing words and so many are misspelled

We rip our hair out in frustration in our seats

Sometimes we don't even want to finish it

Just want to scrap it all and get rid of it

We keep going back trying to fix this mess

The more we do the time we have is less

Life is like a rough draft

No matter how shitty it is there's no point in starting over

As the clock ticks you know you have no choice but to move forward

Can't stop now or else you'll lose all motivation

Trying to ignore everything that's bad like a new station

26.

I wonder when I'll meet you

With my past will you even see this through

I want to see your eyes light up when you see me

I want the butterflies and stumbling

I want the late night talks after making love

To have someone stand by me when push comes to shove

I'm tired of catching myself after I fall in love

All I want is the company of someone I can trust

Don't worry I'm not pushing I'm not in a rush

I just can't seem to find you anywhere

I thought by now I would of settles down

I just want you and I don't want to go around

Can you hear my heart calling you

All i"m getting in response is a busy tone and I feel like a fool

27.

I'm not sure when it was that I died

When the old me was starting to subside

I didn't even get the chance to mourn her

To hold her so close and tell her goodbye

There's so many things that I wish I had said

Now I look in the mirror and she's dead

When it was that I took over

Maybe when I decided not to be sober

She has been through so much

From violent hurricanes to gentle touch

She had such a kind heart and the world took it over

Now this body is the only thing left to show of her

My smile and laugh is definitely different

Probably because half of the time I'm belligerent

The worst part now that she's gone is that I don't even miss her

God how I wish I could change

There comes an end to songs they sing

28.

Never thought you would be the one to talk shit

To think I wanted to get closer then I got hit

Forced to remember why I stay to myself

Begrudgingly I put who I am back on the shelf

This whole entire people thing isn't going to workout

Always giving those who I shouldn't the benefit of the doubt

29.

Swimming In my head with the help of an empty bottle

This lump in my throat that I can't manage to swallow

Wondering what turn I took to get here

Regretting all the choices I made these past years

My head a confessional

As I tell it all my fears

I can't anymore stress

As I'm overwhelmed with endless tears

Waiting for the day I'm free from this mess

Until then I'm stuck with this weight upon my chest

30.

Go ahead and take the bite of the apple

I promise you you won't taste the poison

I disguised myself hiding away the jackal

And as you reach forward I see you moisten your lips

31.

I know this isn't the life for me

Yet i'm not sure if I should keep going

So used to being damaged

Healing is now scary

I'm used to wasted opportunities

To hurting you before you hurt me

Losing control of my life

Making reds lines

Blowing through every single stop sign

I know I'm a burden but I'm worth it

Used to being the regret

These are the accomplishments I've set

I'm not saying Im better off dead

The irony because of the life I've led

I maybe living but I'm not alive

Looking into the mirror I ask myself why

Only for my reflection to remain silent

With no answer or advice to give

My mind filled with what if's

Drowning me in darkness unable to find the switch

Turn on the light

So I can see the destruction of my life

Turn on the light

Because the way I'm walking there's no path in sight

There's a pain I can't even describe

Numbing it with whatever I prescribe

There's a weight I can't shake

I feel it on my chest whenever I wake

I carry it adding more everyday

Pain turns into pleasure that's what I say

The faith I have in myself is starting to expire

Every moment in life seems as if I pull the tower

32.

Everyday feels like day one

Every repeat makes me feel as if you've won

Everyday is a battle

Some of those days I get the sword

Don't believe my promises because I'm not sure if I can even keep my

word

Honestly there's times when I don't even think it's that bad

Just another negative thing about me you wanted to add

I'm even keeping up with my responsibilities

I even met a new happier version of me

Don't you see

This to me is living

That bottle you hate so much makes me breathe

I gave up drugs and I kept the one thing that couldn't chain me

It's not that I have a problem

It's that every drink brings me closer to being free

What do you mean you don't like change

I'm on top of the world there's nothing to rearrange

I am absolutely the on in control

I'll show you I'll just drink it slow

I'll limit it to the weekends

I'll show you that I don't always have to binge

This old door is still holding on by the hinge

The truth is that I give in to temptation when it comes around

I can't even remember this morning I too blacked out

I lied and said I was cold when I began to shake

I keep throwing up trying to remember when I last ate

It's my obsession

You can see it on my face

You can smell it on my breath no matter how hard the wind takes it away

It's the rotating liquor stores

Losing days not knowing the date

It's the irritability the anxiety

Wondering where my money went

That sinking feeling of realizing were it was spent

It's the ovi and going to jail

I didn't even hear the bang when I fell

33.

Loving you is like riding the h train

When i'm with you I feel high even though you take me low

The way you make me feel is inhumane

Up or down it's okay as long as there's another row

There's chips in this stained glass window

So I let you fill in with tempered glass

Let you loving me fill in the cracks

You can be my hot shot

While your knife is in my back

Just another mouse stuck in one of your traps

How can morphine also feel pain

I thought this was love but perhaps

It's just the addiction making me go insane

It's your love your body the craving

Every single time

I come back begging on my knees

I can't hide it the truth is out

For you I am a fiend

Give me more give me more give me more

How can you watch me suffer while I'm in need

How have you gotten so complacent

Especially when my demise is so guaranteed

You said you'll love me like no one else did before

Is this what you meant

Is this what we signed off on

What we agreed

Your touch your lips like fent

And like the south no matter how hard I try I can't concede

Why the fuck won't you let go of me

34.

To be the leaf in the wind

Something so simple

To be lifted

To be carried away

To float away

35.

Fuck me like you hate me

Don't even bother trying to save me

Rip me like a rag doll

It's what I want when all else fails

Can't love myself so do it for me

With every touch I feel dirty and disgusting

Taste the sweet numb vile in my mouth

As you're fucking me

Make my skin crawl when I feel your hands grabbing my jaw

Treat me like I'm worth nothing

That's how I know you care about me

With you is the only time I'm not I'm not drugged for fun

Hit me like an enemy

Knowing I'll return to thee

Seeking dominance is what I need

Grip me tight so I can't breathe

I want you to make me feel filthy

36.

Woman

Pregnant

Baby

Girl

Daughter

Love

Hugs

Dresses

Hair

Barrettes

Older

Pads

Tampons

Shaving

Deodorant

Covered

Lessons

Older

Misunderstandings

Yelling

Arguing

Fighting

Silence

Talking

Fighting

Jealousy

Miscommunicating

Stubborn

Angry

Regret

Remorse

Talking

Relationship

grown

Distant

Love

Marriage

Sex

Pregnant

Baby

Girl

Daughter

Repeat

37.

Oh so you thought I was stuck on you

You thought you could put me in hell like I can't move through

After I walked through the fire I was done with you

You miss me so much and baby that's cool

Trust me when I tell you I've been movedCame out of hell with a polished

shine

Ready to take my power back and claim the world as mine

Don't beg for me back

Because I'm going to make you fall in live

You think you're going to win

Baby check the signs

I've moved on and I'm doing just fine

I'm at the top where I should of been the entire time

And next time you try to come for me you better bring a bigger knife

You thought I was ignorant and stupid

However I'm not the one that lost me you did

38.

I want to lick the stars

Feel the wetness of your hearth

That taste so sweet

Forever on my lips I wish to keep

Feel my mouth on yours

I want to feel you purr

Absolute darkness in which I stir

Digging deep in the sea

My mouth filling up with greed

I caused a storm

And I intend to see how it plays out

Don't give in don't tap out

Won't stop; until the fith round

Don'ty bury it let the scream out

In a way this is a dream

Oh how I love you and me

Every rise of the tide

Let me in let your body confide

You are mine

Not just in this moment

You are mine

Not just in this moment

You are mine

With every touch of torment

To taste the stars and see the shine

I won't be gentle but I'll be kind

39.

How could I be so selfish

I took the boat down with you in it

Too busy flooding in sin

Forgetting that I wasn't the only one who knew how to swim

I know I need to get us out

I'm not sure how I can face the truth

Especially when you counted on me to get you through

I hope this is something I can fix

This hard lesson has to stick

I was too busy focusing on the mist

Now I might lose everything what a stupid risk

40.

I don't know what to think when I look at you

Are we having fun

Or am I a fool

We might dance and twirl

Both knowing what we know

It's been years

And my eyes haven't left you

You feel cold to the touch

My insides coming to life in a rush

Dancing with you feels like russian roulette

Knowing that one dance will soon be left

You tempt me with all your flavors

Charming to the most innocent of cravers

Not many left to tale the tale of something so cancerous

You truly are the devil in disguise

Promising everyone you dance with a high

To think it"ll only cost us one thing

Our lives

You'll break me and I'll die

Because without you I already feel like I'm on that ride

Have you ever tried to escape you

It's like dancing with tied shoes

And everytime I trip

41.

I've made too many bad decisions

So I don't trust easi;y

I've hurt a few people

Not as many that have hurt me

I stay to myself

I tell everyone I like the peace

I stay to myself

The truth is that I am lonely

I'm as lonely as I am angry

I'm as angry as I am hurt

And sometimes I forget those feelings are there

Until it rises in me and it takes over leaving me thoughtless

I can feel logic trying to reach me

However it stays at the border

The more I try to reach it

The more it retreats

Then all 'm left with is another bad decision

42.

Did you see it

Were you even aware

The moment my world tilted

Knocked off its axis to embrace the sun

I don't know when I began to shift

When I started to become the person no one could hit

You thought I wouldn't be able to get up

You begin to build up a tolerance when you drink from a poisonous cup

It was in the pain I changed

It was in the pain i gathered strength

It was in the pain that I found the way

What doesn't kill you makes you stronger

What doesn't kill you makes you stronger

What doesn't kill you turns you into a martyr

And I have sacrificed everything from my old life

I loved myself enough to let the old me go

I will never let anyone win

It's me versus me and it always has been

43.

She lost herself in him

Lost in love and everything that he gave

And when he went away she searched every corner of the earth

She searches for them and refused to give up

She left no rock unturned

No mountain undiscovered and she combed through every inch of the sea

After she inspected every blade of grass she cried

Fore she then knew that he was gone

44.

I don't even know you

Yet you make my palms sweat

Don't even know you

Still I think about the first time our eyes met

This could be the beginning of a story

One that's not disappointing

A book written specifically for you and me

That ends with a happy ending

Baby my nerves are tingling

Love songs I'm on the verge of singing

As I start to flock to thee

Listen to how my heart skip beats

Like a bad drummer skipping beats

Do you feel it too

The connection when I spoke to you

I know

Strange it seems

But what else could this mean

I'm ready to take this leap

And fall where we're meant to be

45.

Constantly losing to the current no matter how strong I row

I'm ready to give up the fight and let it go

I've been through enough and I will beg no more

As the tide goes so will I

I'll let it drift me away like a sleep filled night

46.

The thing is

I don't care if you're remorseful

If your heart is full of regret

Because mine is full of sorrow

Over words that could of simply not of been said

47.

I'll let you explore me for tonight

Don't get attached I only need some healing

So I promise you I'll be yours for the night

I don't care who you are

Or where you came from

As long as you're up to the fight

To twist in sheets that aren't mine

To give myself to another that feels more than right

This desire

This wanting

This needsing has me on fire tonight

That I'm capable of giving such pleasure

To be explored like a diamond

A treasure

To be licked and touched just right

I don't want to pretend

I know we're not together

And after this we'll be less than friends

But baby give it all to me

I promise you I can take it in

Tell me you love me

That I'm perfect

That no one could ever be deserving

Treat me like I'm more than worthy

As you torture me

And leave me squirming

48.

You said we we're too different

But that isn't true

If i cut you there you would bleed the same

How could you let these memories fade away

We've both made a few lefts

We've both strayed

I don't care if they call this toxic

No one knows the love we share

It's just another empty bottle and broken mirror

We're meant to be together it's so clear

These bruises are my pride

Through it all you stuck by my side when so many others have went

We can do this together

How can this relationship be so easy for you to sevior

49.

I bet she was good to you

Was it everything you knew

Those kisses must of been so sweet

For you to be so bold

Did you enjoy those kisses

As much as you enjoyed bringing me pain

I loved you

But for your love for me wasn't the same

Have you always been this way

When was it I missed the change

How did it feel when she was blowing you

And I was the one that fell off of the stage

Was she better than I was

Even though I sacrificed my own pleasure so you could have your way

Disgusted that I let you in

And shamed that I let you touch me in all those ways

How can you look at me

Knowing that I let you touch me in all those ways

I was so naive when it came to you

Everything I see has now changed

The way I see how you look at me

The way you see through

I'm nothing but a child and you're playing pretend

The game is over and there's nothing left for me except for the bitter end

It was the truth for me

Thinking it would set me free

I was so foolish so naive

How could I possibly think that you were just with me

50.

You were my hero

A herp that bled violence with every step

The hero that kissed my scraped knees and bruises

One that told me every night before bed that I love you

To me you were the best so sweet

For my mom you were the monster she was too scared to flee

For sometimes you were the monster that went went bump in the night

Holding my breath and closing my eyes

The yelling was comforting never a surprise

A place where love doesn't roam

A place called home

51.

I'm getting up

I'm tired not wiped out

I hope you enjoyed all my traumas

I know I did

I hope no one can relate to the things in this book but I ow that for some

who pick this up

That won't be the case

Just know you're tougher than what you've been through

Even if you don't want to be

Until part 2 then…